Rain Forest Animals

Written by DEBORAH HODGE
Illustrated by PAT STEPHENS

Kids Can Press

For Alexandra, a huge fan of the rain forest and its animals! – D.H.

For Caitlin – P.S.

I would like to gratefully acknowledge the expert review of the manuscript and art by Dr. Diane Srivastava, Associate Professor (Ecology), Zoology Department, University of British Columbia, Vancouver, BC. Thanks also to Dr. Reese Halter, conservation biologist and founder of Global Forest Science.

A special thank you to my editor, Stacey Roderick, for her many insightful comments and suggestions. It was a great pleasure to work collaboratively with her in creating this series. Thank you also to editors Sheila Barry and Lisa Tedesco for their valuable help in the final stages of this book.

Kids Can Press acknowledges the financial support of the Government of Ontario, through the Ontario Media Development Corporation's Ontario Book Initiative; the Ontario Arts Council; the Canada Council for the Arts; and the Government of Canada, through the BPIDP, for our publishing activity.

Published in Canada by
Kids Can Press Ltd
29 Birch Avenue
Toronto, ON M4V 1E2

Published in the U.S. by
Kids Can Press Ltd.
2250 Military Road
Tonawanda, NY 14150

www.kidscanpress.com

Kids Can Press is a l𝑜𝑟𝑢𝑠™ Entertainment company

Edited by Stacey Roderick
Designed by Céleste Gagnon and Katie Gray
Printed and bound in Singapore

The hardcover edition of this book is smyth sewn casebound.
The paperback edition of this book is limp sewn with a drawn-on cover.

CM 08 0 9 8 7 6 5 4 3 2 1
CM PA 08 0 9 8 7 6 5 4 3 2 1

Library and Archives Canada Cataloguing in Publication
Hodge, Deborah
    Rain forest animals / written by Deborah Hodge ; illustrated by Pat Stephens.

(Who lives here?)
ISBN 978-1-55453-041-0 (bound)
ISBN 978-1-55453-042-7 (pbk.)

1. Rain forest animals—Juvenile literature. I. Stephens, Pat, 1950-
I. Title. III. Series: Hodge, Deborah. Who lives here?

QL112.H63 2008   j591.734   C2007-902961-2

Contents

What Is a Rain Forest?

A rain forest is a warm, wet place. Rain falls here almost every day. The sun shines on the forest all year long. Most rain forests are found in hot parts of the world.

A rain forest is full of fantastic animals. Their bodies are built for living among the tall trees and lush green plants.

Fruit and nuts grow on many rain forest trees. This parrot is gobbling up a wild cherry. Yummy!

Thick vines twist and grow between the trees. Small animals scamper through the forest along the vines.

Big, bright flowers catch the falling rain. They are like bowls of water for thirsty monkeys and birds.

5

Orangutan

The orangutan is the biggest animal in the world to live in a tree. It climbs through the rain forest, searching for fruit.

Orangutans live alone, except for mothers who have babies. A baby holds on tight to its mother's fur as they travel.

Long, powerful arms hold up the orangutan's heavy body as it swings through the trees.

Slurp! An orangutan uses its big hand like a cup to scoop up a drink of rainwater.

A sleepy orangutan makes its bed in a tree. A roof of leafy branches helps keep out the rain. Zzz ...

Toucan

The toucan is a bird that lives high in the treetops of the rain forest. Some toucans are as big as large cats.

A heavy toucan perches on a strong branch and uses its long beak to reach berries growing on thinner branches. Delicious!

8

Toucans have four toes on each foot. Two toes point backward and two toes point forward for a tight grip.

A toucan makes its nest in a hole in a tree. This baby toucan hatched in the nest.

A toucan's beak is like a sharp knife. It has jagged edges for cutting up big pieces of fruit.

9

Howler Monkey

The howler monkey is one of the loudest animals in the rain forest. The monkey's howl sounds like a deep roar.

Howler monkeys live in groups, high in the tall trees. Monkeys in one group howl, or call out, to warn other groups to stay away.

A howler monkey has a hollow bone in its neck. Its voice echoes inside the bone and becomes very loud. Roar!

This hungry monkey uses its strong tail to hold itself up while searching for leaves and fruit to eat.

A baby howler monkey clings tightly to its mother. Babies purr softly instead of howling.

Tapir

The tapir has a round body like a rhinoceros. Tapirs live near the rivers, lakes and streams of the rain forest.

A tapir swims and splashes in the water to cool off. If a hungry jaguar comes near, the tapir will dive down and hide.

A tapir uses its snout like a snorkel to breathe when the rest of its body is hidden underwater.

Sniff, sniff, sniff. A tapir's snout moves back and forth to find leaves, branches, plants and fruit to eat.

A baby's striped fur blends in with the light and shadows of the forest. This helps it hide from jaguars and other enemies.

Emerald Tree Boa

The emerald tree boa is a long, strong snake that slithers through the rain forest trees.

Shh ... The boa waits silently on a branch. It is watching for its prey — the birds and other small animals it eats.

An emerald tree boa hangs by its tail so its mouth is free to grab a bird flying by.

A boa wraps itself around its prey, squeezing it very tightly. When the animal dies, the boa swallows it whole.

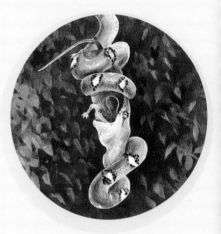

A baby's red skin will turn green as it gets older. Its green skin helps the boa hide in the trees and surprise its prey.

Jaguar

The jaguar is a big, fierce cat that prowls through the rain forest. Jaguars hunt on land, in water and even in trees!

From a hiding spot in the forest, a jaguar quietly watches. When a tapir, deer or other animal comes near, the jaguar will pounce!

A jaguar's spotted fur blends in with the colors of the forest and helps it hide.

Jaguars kill their prey with one bite. Their strong jaws and sharp teeth can break through animal bones. Crunch!

This thirsty jaguar cub takes a cool drink from the river's edge. Like all jaguars, it will be a very good swimmer.

17

Gorilla

The gorilla lives on the ground, deep inside the rain forest. Gorillas are too big to have their homes up in the trees.

A gorilla travels in a family group made up of mothers, babies, young gorillas and a male leader. They eat, sleep and play together.

The leader scares enemies away by running at them or beating on his chest like a drum. Boom, boom, boom!

A gorilla walks on its feet and the knuckles of its hands. This is called "knuckle-walking."

This hungry gorilla picks tasty plants with its big hands. Gorillas gobble up leaves, shoots, stems and fruit.

Sloth

The sloth is the slowest animal in the rain forest. Sloths are asleep or very still most of the time.

A sloth spends much of its day hanging upside down in a tree. A mother sloth eats, sleeps and gives birth to her baby here.

A sloth's long, curved claws hook onto branches to keep it from falling.

When a hungry sloth has eaten the tender leaves and shoots from one tree, it will s-l-o-w-l-y move to another tree.

Sloths are very good swimmers, but they can't walk. On land, a sloth drags its body forward with its long claws.

Red-Eyed Tree Frog

The red-eyed tree frog lives in the trees of the rain forest, sleeping by day and hunting by night.

The frog climbs through the trees, searching for insects to eat. Its bright red eyes startle enemies that come near.

Sticky pads on the frog's toes work like little suction cups. They make it easy to climb up wet leaves and branches.

With skin the color of a bright green leaf, the frog can hide from hungry snakes and birds.

Boing! A tree frog leaps away on its strong, long legs to escape an enemy.

23

Animal Words

Every rain forest animal has special body parts that help it get food and stay safe. Can you find pictures of these body parts in the book?

beak
page 9

claws
page 21

fur
page 17

hands
page 19

snout
page 13

toes
page 23

For Parents and Teachers

Tropical rain forests occur in regions of the world that are near the equator and have year-round warm temperatures and abundent rainfall. These lush forests are home to an amazing diversity of animal species. Orangutans live in rain forests in Southeast Asia, while gorillas are found in Africa. Tapirs live in both Asia and the Americas. The other animals in this book are found either in Central America, South America or both. Some also live in southern Mexico.

Today, South America is home to the largest area of rain forest left in the world. Sadly, as more rain forests are being cleared for farms, ranches and roads, there is less space for animals to live. This loss of habitat leads to some species, such as the gorilla, becoming endangered.